D1062649

WILD AGE

SEA MONSTERS

STEVE PARKER

QEB Publishing

Project Editor: Carey Scott
Designer: Stefan Morris Design
Illustrations: The Art Agency and MW Digital Graphics

Picture Researcher: Maria Joannou

Library of Congress Cataloging-in-Publication Data
Parker, Steve, 1952-
    Sea monsters / Steve Parker.
        p. cm. -- (QEB wild age)
    Includes index.
    ISBN 978-1-59566-914-8 (lib. bdg.)
    1. Paleontology--Paleozoic--Juvenile literature. 2. Paleontology--Mesozoic-
-Juvenile literature. 3. Paleontology--Tertiary--Juvenile literature. 4. Marine
mammals, Fossil--Juvenile literature. I. Title.
    QE725.P37 2011
    560--dc22   2010001155

ISBN 978-1-59566-914-8

Printed in China

Copyright © QEB Publishing, Inc. 2010

Published in the United States by
QEB Publishing, Inc.
3 Wrigley, Suite A
Irvine, CA 92618

www.qed-publishing.co.uk

Picture credits

Key: t=top, b=bottom, r=right, l=left, c=centre
Alamy Images John Cancalosi 7t, 28cr (redlichia),
Melba Photo Agency 18-19, 30br; **Corbis** Jonathan Blair 21t, Mike Nelson/EPA 26-27,
Visuals Unlimited 28cl (ophiura), 28cr (pterygotus), 29cl (cephalaspis), Peter Visscher
4br, Jon Hughes 5cl (ichthyosaur), 5bl, 20-21, 29br, Giuliano Fornari 30cl (archelon); **FLPA** Norbert Wu/
Minden Pictures 19t, 29cl (coelacanth); **Getty Images** Dorling Kindersley 5cl (plesiosaur), 14-15, 22-23,
29cr (kronosaurus), 29bl, Visuals Unlimited/Gerald & Buff Corsi 13tr, Visuals Unlimited/Ken Lucas 25b;
Istockphoto Dawn Hagan 3b, Breckeni 5br, Asterix0597 30cr (parapuzosia); **Photolibrary** De Agostini
Editore 4bl, 5cr (early whale), 6-7b, 16-17, 28tl, 30tr, 30cl (basilosaurus), 30cr (mosasaurus), SGM SGM 1pl,
28bl; **Photoshot** NHPA/Andrea Ferrari 23t, 30bl; **Science Photo Library** Christian Jegou Publiphoto
Diffusion 4cl, 5tr, 12-13, 28tr, Richard Bizley 4cr, 10-11, 29cr (megateuthis), Chris Butler 5cr (mososaur), 24-
25, 29tr, Jim Amos 9t, Christian Darkin 15b, 27br, 28cl (climatius), 29tl, 30tl; **Shutterstock** Jim Barber 2t,
Steve Collender 2b, Ryan M. Bolton 3t, M. Dykstra 4bc, SGame 4-5t, 28br,
W. Scott 17t; **Stock Exchange** 1

All maps: **Mark Walker**
MW Digital Graphics

The words in **bold** are
explained in the Glossary
on page 31.

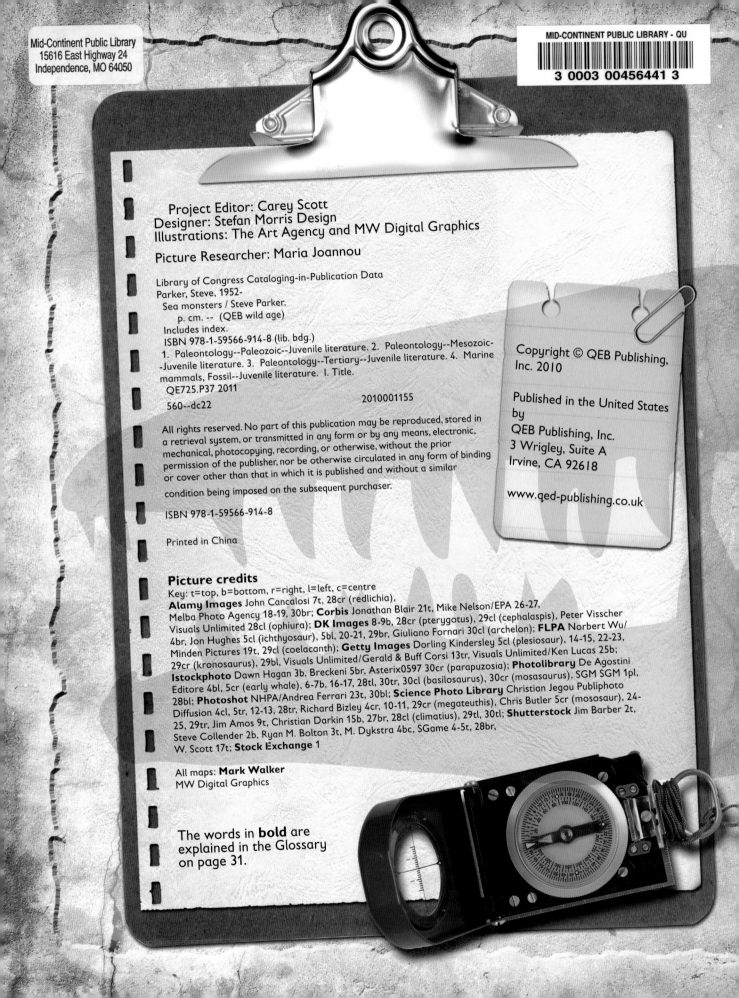

CONTENTS

JELLY MONSTERS

The first living things began in the oceans more than 3000 million years ago. They were too tiny to see. Over millions of years they became larger and more complicated—the sea's first mini-monsters.

These early animals had no teeth, legs, or shells. They had soft bodies and looked like today's jellyfish and worms. The biggest were the size of your thumb, such as *Spriggina*.

Such strange creatures probably wriggled along the seabed or drifted in the water. What did they eat? No one really knows. Perhaps mud, or the first seaweeds—or maybe each other!

◗ *Spriggina* had a curved head, lots of body sections called segments, and a narrow tail.

⬭ **Prehistoric time** is divided into periods, which have their own names. Each period started and ended a certain number of millions of years ago (mya).

510 mya

The first fish appear

First ammonites

410 mya

Ediacaran	Cambrian	Ordovician	Silurian	Devonian	Carboniferous	Permian
before 542 mya	542–488 mya	488–444 mya	444–416 mya	416–359 mya	359–299 mya	299–251 mya

550 mya   500 mya   400 mya   300 mya

540 mya Shelled sea animals   **460 mya** Land plants   **430 mya** Tiny land animals   **360 mya** Four-legged land animals

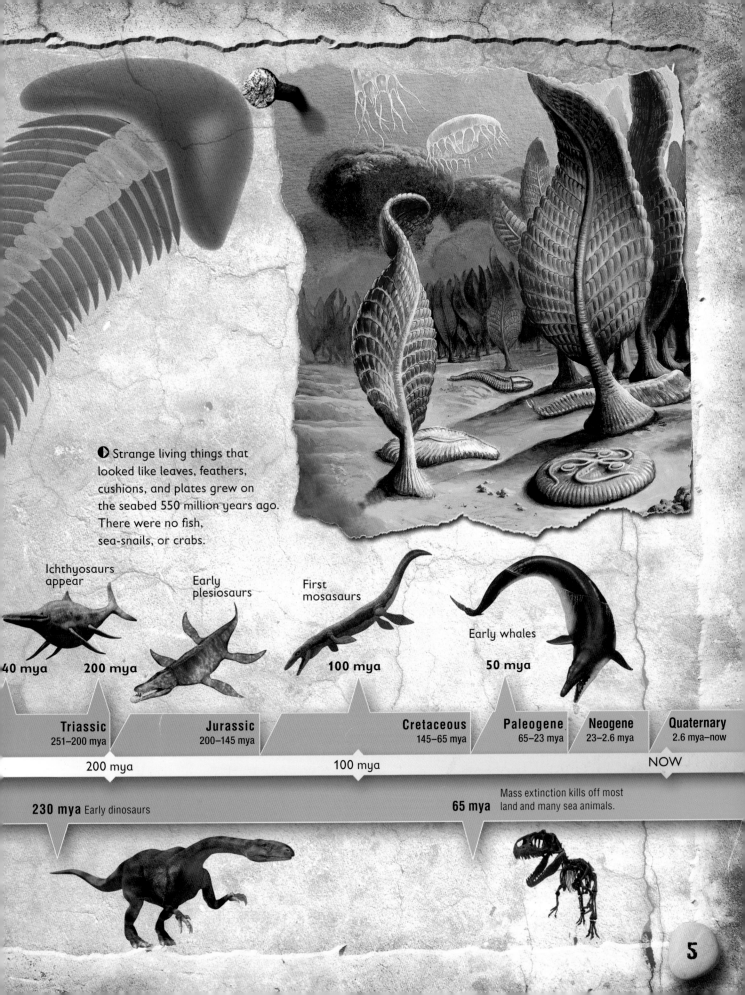

◗ Strange living things that looked like leaves, feathers, cushions, and plates grew on the seabed 550 million years ago. There were no fish, sea-snails, or crabs.

Ichthyosaurs appear

Early plesiosaurs

First mosasaurs

Early whales

40 mya   **200 mya**   **100 mya**   **50 mya**

Triassic 251–200 mya	**Jurassic** 200–145 mya	**Cretaceous** 145–65 mya	**Paleogene** 65–23 mya	**Neogene** 23–2.6 mya	**Quaternary** 2.6 mya–now

200 mya   **100 mya**   NOW

230 mya Early dinosaurs

65 mya Mass extinction kills off most land and many sea animals.

SHIELD SHELLS

About 530 million years ago, many new animals appeared in the seas. Most were small but fierce, and they had a new feature—a shell!

Shells protected their wearers against enemies. Once the animals died, their shells formed **fossils**—remains of once-living things, preserved in the rocks and turned to stone.

The largest hunter of the time, *Anomalocaris*, was probably bigger than you! It swam by waving its fan-shaped tail and side flaps, and it grabbed **prey** with its two long spiked "arms." Its round mouth had many teeth to pull in and chew up its meal.

WILD FILE

Anomalocaris

GROUP Anomalocaridid

WHEN Cambrian Period

FOOD Hard-shelled creatures

FOSSIL SITES North America including Canada, China, Australia

● Fossil sites

● Watching with its two big eyes, *Anomalocaris* pushes a smaller creature into its round mouth using its two feeding arms.

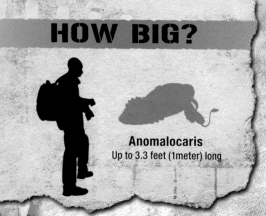

HOW BIG?

Anomalocaris
Up to 3.3 feet (1meter) long

◑ **Trilobites** such as *Redlichia* were among the first animals to have eyes, and strong shells—especially over the head end.

WILD!

Until 1985, scientists thought that fossils of separate parts of *Anomalocaris* were from three different animals—a jellyfish, a sponge, and a shrimp.

SCORPIONS OF THE SEA

About 420 million years ago, giant scorpions became the seas' rulers. They were some of the most powerful predators of their time.

Sea scorpions did not have a poison tail sting like today's land scorpions. But they did have big eyes to see their prey, and two very strong pincers to grab a victim and tear it apart.

Sea scorpions could crawl about on their eight legs, and were able to breathe air like some of today's crabs. They could also swim by swishing their paddle-like rear legs to move and their fan-shaped tail to steer.

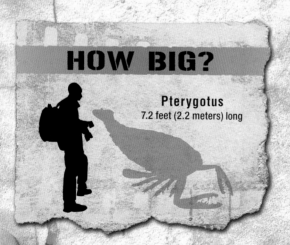

HOW BIG?

Pterygotus
7.2 feet (2.2 meters) long

WILD FILE

Pterygotus

GROUP Sea-scorpions (Eurypterids)

WHEN Late Silurian

FOOD Fish

WHERE Worldwide, especially North America and Europe

● Fossil sites

◑ Brittle stars are types of bendy-armed starfish. As long as 450 million years ago they covered the seabed in huge numbers, eating tiny bits of food in the mud.

CLOSE COUSINS

Sea-scorpions were members of the **arachnid** group—cousins of today's scorpions and spiders as well as mites, ticks, and horseshoe or king crabs.

◓ The huge nippers of *Pterygotus* could stab and tear apart almost any creature of the time—including its own young.

CURLS AND CONES

The first curly-shelled ammonites hunted in the seas about 400 million years ago. They swam fast by squirting out a jet of water, just like today's squid.

An **ammonite**'s shell shape is called a spiral. As the ammonite grew, it made a new, wider section at the shell's open end. This became the ammonite's home. It had big eyes and more than 20 tentacles to grab its prey.

Belemnites were similar to ammonites, but most had ten tentacles and a body shaped like an ice-cream cone. Some belemnites were as long as a family car!

WILD!

Belemnites had a small shell completely hidden inside the body. It was rod-shaped and pointed at one end, like a bullet. These fossil shells are called "belemnite bullets."

◐ These are fossils of shells from *Orthoceras*, a creature called a **nautiloid**. It looked like a long, straight ammonite.

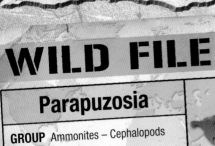

● *Parapuzosia's* main body was inside the end of its coiled shell. If the ammonite was in danger, it could hide its tentacles in the shell too, in the same way that snails pull themselves into their shells.

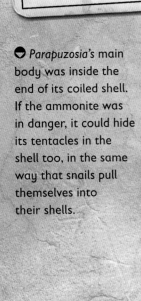

FIRST FISH

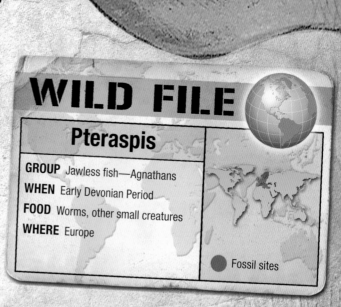

Today, there are millions of fishes in the sea. But, until about 510 million years ago, there were no fish at all.

The first fish had no jaws in their mouth so they could not bite and chew. The mouth was probably a thin slit or rounded opening, through which the fish sucked in its food.

These **jawless fish** did not have movable fins like later fish, but their streamlined bodies enabled them to swim well. They were protected from predators by a hard head shield and bony scales along the back. Some could live in the sea and swim into rivers too.

WILD FILE

Pteraspis

GROUP	Jawless fish—Agnathans
WHEN	Early Devonian Period
FOOD	Worms, other small creatures
WHERE	Europe

Fossil sites

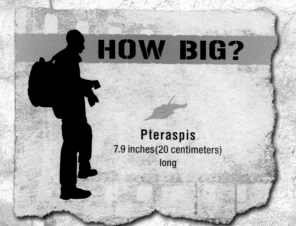

HOW BIG?

Pteraspis
7.9 inches (20 centimeters)
long

WILD!

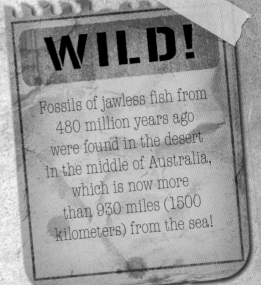

Fossils of jawless fish from 480 million years ago were found in the desert in the middle of Australia, which is now more than 930 miles (1500 kilometers) from the sea!

◓ Two kinds of jawless fish still exist today – lampreys and hagfish. They suck blood and scrape flesh from other animals. The hagfish is soft and pink and it can cover itself with its own thick slime in a few seconds.

◐ The early fish, *Pteraspis*, with its nose and back horns, swims along at the top of this ancient sea scene. Lower left is one of its jawless cousins, *Arandaspis*.

MONSTERS IN THE DEEP

As more fish appeared in the seas, some kinds grew larger. One of the biggest was Dunkleosteus, which was as long as a bus.

Dunkleosteus had thick armor plates of bone over its head and neck for protection. The rest of its body was probably not well protected. But a fish this huge had few enemies!

The teeth of *Dunkleosteus* were fearsome sharp blades of bone. They could easily slice through the armor of other **hard-bodied animals**.

HOW BIG?

Dunkleosteus
32.8 feet (10 meters) long

● *Dunkleosteus* weighed more than 3 tons, which is four times heavier than today's great white shark. Its bite was as powerful as that of the dinosaur *Tyrannosaurus rex*.

WILD!

Some fossils of *Dunkleosteus* have bite marks from the teeth of other *Dunkleosteus*. So these massive fish were probably cannibals – they ate each other!

WILD FILE

Dunkleosteus

GROUP Armored fish – Placoderms

WHEN Late Devonian Period

FOOD Sharks, other fish, ammonites

FOSSIL SITES North Africa, Europe, North America

● Fossil sites

◗ *Bothriolepsis* had bony body armor, like *Dunkleosteus*. This fish was only 11.8 inches (30 centimeters) long. It probably lived in rivers, not in the sea.

SHARK GIANTS

True sharks appeared more than 400 million years ago, and all were fierce hunters. Spiny sharks were another group of early fish.

Spiny sharks were not really sharks, but they did have shark-like streamlined bodies and sharp spines. They had thorns in their fins and skin to prevent predators eating them. They probably ate fish, shellfish, and worms.

The biggest of the **true sharks** was *Megalodon*, which hunted in the seas until about 1.5 million years ago.

It was similar to today's great white—but three times longer and 20 times heavier!

WILD FILE

Megalodon

GROUP Sharks – Selachians
WHEN Neogene Period
FOOD Large sea animals
WHERE Worldwide

• Fossil sites

● *Megalodon* had more than 250 huge, razor-sharp teeth. The fossils of its teeth were once thought to be the tongues of dragons or similar beasts.

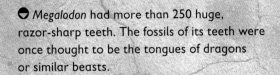
CLOSE COUSINS

Megalodon was in the same shark group as today's great white shark, mako shark, and porbeagle shark. All of these are big, fast, fierce hunters—just like their prehistoric relative.

● The mouth of *Megalodon* was so huge that it could easily swallow a person. Every week its old, worn-out or broken teeth fell out, and new ones grew in their place.

FISHY FINS

Gradually, over millions of years, fish developed in different ways to become better, faster swimmers and more efficient hunters.

Some fish grew fins that spread out like fans, for better swimming control. One of the biggest of these was *Xiphactinus*. This fierce predator had pointed fangs up to 3.9 inches (10 centimeters) long.

Other fish, called **lobe-fins**, had fins with fleshy muscular bases. They could use these to crawl across land from one pool to another. Gradually some of them became the first four-legged land animals.

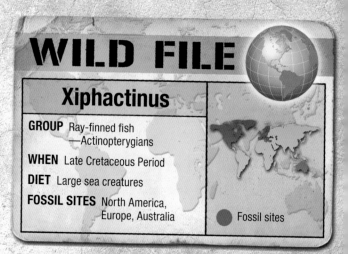

HOW BIG?

Xiphactinus
16.4 feet (5meters) long

Lobe-fin fish called coelacanths lived more than 70 million years ago. Two kinds are still around today, swimming in the deep waters of the Indian Ocean.

Xiphactinus was a long, slim, speedy hunter. It died out with the dinosaurs, 65 million years ago.

WILD!

Inside one fossil of *Xiphactinus* was the fossil of another fish it had just eaten. This fish, *Gillicus*, was 5.9 feet (1.8 meters) long—bigger than you!

SPEEDY KILLERS

While dinosaurs ruled the land, from 230 million years ago, new monsters took over the seas. Fastest were the "fish lizards," the ichthyosaurs.

On the outside, **ichthyosaurs** looked like dolphins. But they were in the same group as dinosaurs—the **reptiles**. They came to the surface to breathe through the mouth or the nostrils (nose-holes) in front of the eyes.

Ichthyosaurs swished their tails from side to side to swim at speeds of up to 25 miles (40 kilometers) an hour. They grabbed their prey in their long, slim jaws.

HOW BIG?

Shonisaurus
65 feet (20 meters) long

Ichthyosaurs might look like dolphins, or fishes, or even crocodiles. But these are not close relatives. Their nearest cousins are lizards and snakes in the reptile group.

◖ The first complete ichthyosaur fossil to be discovered was named *Ichthyosaurus*. It was quite small, just 6.5 feet (2 meters) long.

◖ The giant ichthyosaur, *Shonisaurus*, was one of the largest hunters that ever lived in the sea. It had a back fin like a dolphin and four flipper-like limbs for steering — dolphins have only two.

NECKS AND FLIPPERS

During the Age of the Dinosaurs, enormous reptiles called plesiosaurs hunted in the oceans. Some had teeth as long as carving knives!

There were two main kinds of **plesiosaurs**, and both swam by flapping their huge flippers. The long-necked types could easily grab fish and other animals to eat up.

Short-necked plesiosaurs, called **pliosaurs**, had a short neck but a massive head and jaws. They were **top predators** and could eat almost any victims, including big fish, sea turtles, ichthyosaurs, and other plesiosaurs.

HOW BIG?

Kronosaurus
32.8 feet (10 meters) long

WILD FILE

Kronosaurus

GROUP Pliosaurs – Short-necked Plesiosaurs

WHEN Early Cretaceous Period

DIET Large sea creatures

FOSSIL SITES Australia, South America

● Fossil sites

● *Elasmosaurus* was 45 feet (14 meters) long, and more than half the length was its neck. It darted out its head like a snake to snap at creaures such as ammonites.

◑ *Kronosaurus* probably swam mainly with its front flippers, using the back ones for bursts of speed. Each tooth was bigger than your hand but fairly blunt, for crushing rather than cutting.

WILD!

Newly discovered fossils known as Predator X may be from the most massive pliosaur ever discovered. This giant could have been 50 feet (15 meters) long and 55 tons in weight.

MOUTHFUL OF TEETH

As plesiosaurs and ichthyosaurs died out, near the end of the Age of the Dinosaurs, a new kind of monster came to rule the seas—the mosasaur.

Mosasaurs were some of the biggest, fastest, strongest ocean hunters ever. Their long jaws were full of sharp cone-shaped teeth, which they used to tear their prey apart.

Like pliosaurs and ichthyosaurs, mosasaurs stayed near the surface to breathe air. They could not walk on land with their flippers. So they stayed in the sea, and even gave birth to their babies there.

HOW BIG?

Mosasaurus
50 feet (15 meters) long

CLOSE COUSINS

Mosasaurs looked similar to crocodiles. But their nearest relatives today are the types of lizards called monitors. This group includes the world's biggest lizard, the Komodo dragon.

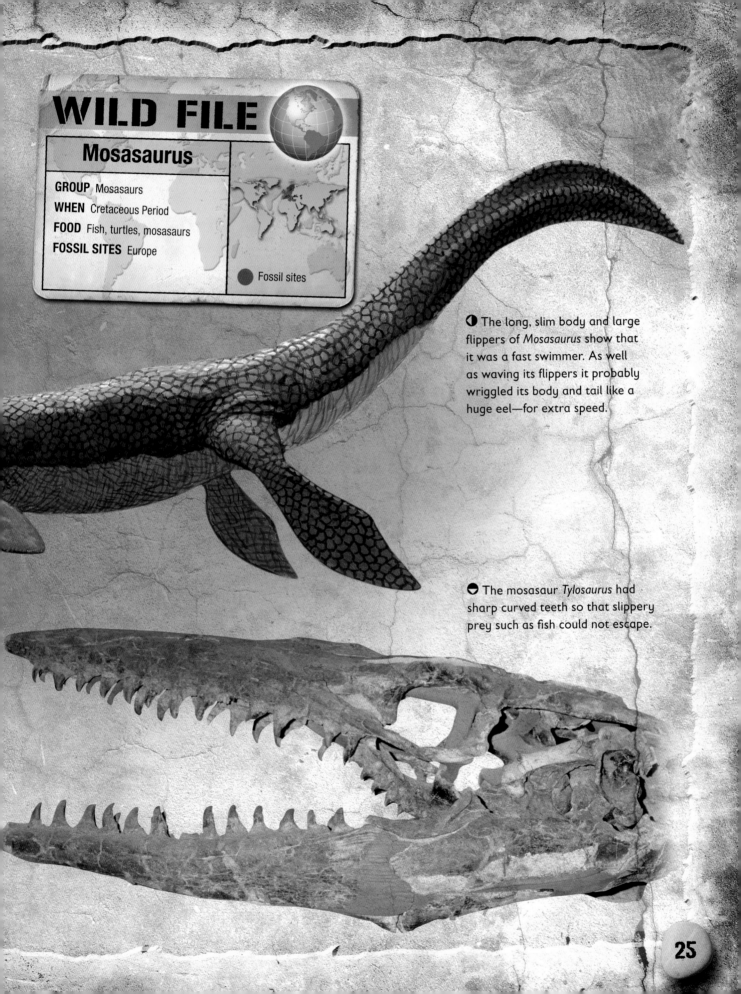

Mosasaurus

GROUP Mosasaurs
WHEN Cretaceous Period
FOOD Fish, turtles, mosasaurs
FOSSIL SITES Europe

● Fossil sites

◖ The long, slim body and large flippers of *Mosasaurus* show that it was a fast swimmer. As well as waving its flippers it probably wriggled its body and tail like a huge eel—for extra speed.

● The mosasaur *Tylosaurus* had sharp curved teeth so that slippery prey such as fish could not escape.

BACK TO THE SEA

Many reptile sea monsters died out along with the dinosaurs, 65 million years ago. Soon their place was taken by mammals that had left the land and gone into the water.

At first, all **mammals** lived on land. By about 55 million years ago some were splashing along the seashore and hunting in the shallows. These were the first whales and dolphins.

Gradually the whales' front legs became flippers. They lost their back legs and grew wide tail flukes for swimming. The whales alive now are the biggest sea creatures of all time.

◗ These fossil experts are digging up the remains of *Basilosaurus*, including its long backbone, from the desert sands of North Africa.

HOW BIG?

Basilosaurus
Up to 82 feet (25 meters) long

WILD FILE

Basilosaurus

GROUP Whales – Cetaceans
WHEN Middle Paleogene Period
FOOD Fish to large sea creatures
WHERE North America, Africa, Asia

● Fossil sites

Ambulocetus was almost a whale and a good swimmer. But it still had four legs so that it could walk on land. Its fossils came from Pakistan in Asia.

WILD GUIDE

Anomalocaris

Pronunciation
an-om-all-owe-carr-is

Meaning Strange shrimp

Group Crabs and shrimps (crustaceans)

Time period Cambrian, 500 million years ago

Size Up to 3.3 feet (1 meter) long

Weight About 18 lbs (8 kg)

Pteraspis

Pronunciation
tear-ass-pis

Meaning Wing shield

Group Jawless fish (agnathans)

Time period Devonian, 400 mya

Size 7.9 in (20 cm) long

Weight About 17.7 oz (500 g)

Climatius

Pronunciation
klime-ate-ee-us

Meaning Zone fish

Group Spiny sharks (acanthodians)

Time period Silurian-Devonian, 420–410 mya

Size 3.2 in (8 cm) long

Weight 8.8 oz (250 g)

Pterygotus

Pronunciation
terry-goat-us

Meaning Winged animal

Group Seascorpions (eurypterids)

Time period Silurian, 420 mya

Size 7.2 ft (2.2 m) long

Weight 154 lbs (70 kg)

Ophiura

Pronunciation
off-ee-ure-a

Meaning Snake tail

Group Brittlestars and starfish (echinoderms)

Time period Ordovician, 480 mya

Size 20 in (50 cm) across

Weight 2.2 lbs (2 kg)

Redlichia

Pronunciation
red-lick-ee-a

Meaning In honour of Hans Redlich

Group Trilobites

Time period Cambrian, 500 mya

Size Up to 20 in (50 cm) long

Weight 6.6 lbs (3 kg)

Orthoceras

Pronunciation
or-thow-sare-ass

Meaning Straight horn

Group Nautiloids (molluscs)

Time period Silurian, 420 mya

Size 6.5 ft (2 m) long

Weight 110 lbs (50 kg)

Spriggina

Pronunciation
sprig-een-a

Meaning In honour of Reg Sprigg

Group Probably worms (annelids)

Time period Ediacaran, 550 mya

Size 1.2 in (3 cm) long

Weight 1 oz (30g)

WILD GUIDE

Bothriolepis

Pronunciation both-ree-owe-lep-iss

Meaning Pitted scale

Group Armored fish (placoderms)

Time period Devonian, 370 mya

Size 11.8 in (30 cm) long

Weight 2.2 lbs (1 kg)

Cephalaspis

Pronunciation seff-al-ass-pis

Meaning Head shield

Group Jawless fish (agnathans)

Time period Devonian, 400 mya

Size 20 in (50 cm) long

Weight About 4 lbs (2 kg)

Coelacanth

Pronunciation seel-ah-kanth

Meaning Hollow spine

Group Lobe-finned fish (sarcopterygians)

Time period Devonian, 400 mya, to today

Size 6.5 ft (2 m) long

Weight 176 lbs (80 kg)

Dunkleosteus

Pronunciation dunk-lee-oss-tee-us

Meaning Dunkle's bone

Group Armored fish (placoderms)

Time period Devonian, 370 mya

Size 3.3 ft (10 m) long

Weight About 2 tons

Ichthyosaurus

Pronunciation ick-thee-owe-saw-rus

Meaning Fish lizard

Group Ichthyosaurs

Time period Early Jurassic, 190 mya

Size 6.5 feet (2 m) long

Weight 165 lbs (75 kg)

Kronosaurus

Pronunciation crow-no-saw-rus

Meaning Time lizard

Group Pliosaurs (short-necked plesiosaurs)

Time period Early Cretaceous, 110 mya

Size 3.3 ft (10 m) long

Weight 10 tons

Megateuthis

Pronunciation meg-a-te-oo-this

Meaning Huge squid

Group Belemnites (molluscs)

Time period Jurassic, 150 mya

Size 9.8 ft (3 m) long

Weight About 176 lbs (80 kg)

Shonisaurus

Pronunciation shon-ee-saw-rus

Meaning Shoshone lizard

Group Ichthyosaurs

Time period Late Triassic, 210 mya

Size 65 ft (20 m) long

Weight 30 tons

WILD GUIDE

Ambulocetus

Pronunciation am-bue-low-seet-us

Meaning Walking whale

Group Whales and dolphins (cetaceans)

Time period Early Paleogene, 50 mya

Size 9.8 ft (3 m)

Weight 440 lbs (200 kg)

Archelon

Pronunciation ark-ee-lon

Meaning Ruler turtle

Group Turtles (chelonians)

Time period Late Cretaceous, 70 mya

Size 13 ft (4 m) long

Weight About 2 tons

Basilosaurus

Pronunciation baz-ill-owe-saw-rus

Meaning Emperor lizard

Group Whales and dolphins (cetaceans)

Time period Mid Paleogene, 35 mya

Size 82 ft (25 m)

Weight 66 tons

Elasmosaurus

Pronunciation ee-laz-mow-saw-rus

Meaning Thin plate

Group Plesiosaurs

Time period Late Cretaceous, 70 mya

Size 45 ft (14 m) long

Weight 2.2 tons

Megalodon

Pronunciation meg-ah-lowe-don

Meaning Huge tooth

Group Sharks (selachians)

Time period Neogene, to 1.5 mya

Size 59 ft (18 m) long

Weight 55 tons

Mosasaurus

Pronunciation mow-za-saw-rus

Meaning Meuse lizard

Group Mosasaurs

Time period Late Cretaceous, 70 mya

Size 50 ft (15 m) long

Weight 22 tonnes

Parapuzosia

Pronunciation para-poo-zow-see-a

Meaning Alongside Puzos

Group Ammonites (molluscs)

Time period Late Cretaceous, 70 mya

Size 8.2 ft (2.5 m) across

Weight About 330 lbs (150 kg)

Xiphactinus

Pronunciation ziff-act-eye-nus

Meaning Sword ray

Group Ray-finned fish (actinopterygians)

Time period Late Cretaceous, 70 mya

Size 16.4 ft (5 m) long

Weight About 1320 lbs (600 kg)

GLOSSARY

Age of the Dinosaurs The time when dinosaurs were the main large land animals, from about 230 to 65 million years ago.

Ammonite A sea creature related to octopus and squid, with big eyes, lots of tentacles, and a curly, snail-like shell. All ammonites have died out, or become extinct.

Arachnid A member of the animal group that includes spiders, scorpions, mites, and ticks.

Belemnite A sea creature related to octopus and squid, with big eyes, lots of tentacles, and usually a cone-shaped shell. Belemnites are extinct now, but they have left many fossils.

Fossil Any part of a plant or animal that has been preserved in rock. Also traces of plants or animals, such as footprints.

Hard-bodied animals Creatures with a hard outer body casing instead of an inside skeleton, such as snails, shellfish, and beetles.

Ichthyosaur A sea-living, air-breathing reptile that looked similar to a dolphin, with paddle-shaped limbs and a swishy tail.

Jawless fish A fish that does not have jaw bones for biting, but usually has a mouth like a sucker or slit.

Lobe-fin fish A fish with fins that have strong muscles in fleshy lumps or lobes at the base.

Mammal An animal that has hair or fur and produces milk for its babies.

Mosasaur A sea-living, air-breathing reptile with paddle-like limbs and a large mouth with many big, sharp teeth.

Nautiloid A sea creature related to octopus and squid, with big eyes, lots of tentacles, and a curly, snail-like shell.

Plesiosaur A sea-living, air-breathing reptile with paddle-shaped limbs, a very long neck, and a small head with small, sharp teeth.

Pliosaur A sea-living, air-breathing reptile with long paddle-shaped limbs, a big head, huge mouth, and sharp teeth.

Prehistoric time The time up to several thousand years ago, before people started to write down what happened as recorded history.

Prey A creature that is killed and eaten by another animal, the predator.

Ray-finned fish A fish with fins that have long, thin rods or rays holding them out. The rays can move to change the fin's shape.

Reptile A scaly, usually cold-blooded animal, such as a lizard, snake, crocodile, turtle, dinosaur, ichthyosaur, mosasaur, or plesiosaur.

Spiny sharks Fish that looked like sharks, with sharp spines on their bodies for protection, but which were not in the main shark group.

Top predator A big hunting animal that can kill and eat most other creatures, and which no other animal would attack and eat.

Trilobite A sea-living creature with big eyes, a hard upper body shell, and many pairs of legs underneath.

True sharks Fish in the group that scientists call selachians, with a skeleton made, not of bone, but of cartilage or gristle.

INDEX